THE REALLY Amazing ANIMAL BOOK

Animal Athletes
Pages 8-9

Record
Breakers
Pages 20-21

Baby Beasts
Pages 18-19

Hearty
Appetites
Pages 12-13

DK

DORLING KINDERSLEY
LONDON • NEW YORK • STUTTGART • MOSCOW

Skin, Spikes, and Smells

The animal kingdom can be a tough and dangerous place, so animals have many different ways to stay alive. Some are built like tanks or possess nasty weapons.

How do animals protect themselves?

Extra-thick skin

An Indian rhino's leathery skin is like a suit of armour. All animals, from ticks to tigers, have difficulty biting into it.

This rhino's skin hangs in folded sheets.

Did you know? Rhinos' horns are made of stuck-together hair.

Indian rhino's short, worn-down horn

Stingers

Larger predators stay clear of this lionfish. Its stinging spines can disable or kill other creatures.

Poisonous spines

An animal that hunts and eats another animal is called a **predator**.

Tiny tanks

Tiny insects need armour for protection. Most beetles have hard wing cases. These put off predators because they are tough and difficult to eat.

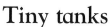

Hard wing case ——

Its tail slots into a special fold.

Smelly surprise

A skunk's weapon in a fight is the smelly spray it releases from under its tail. This spray can cause temporary blindness.

A tusk can weigh more than a man.

Mud baths coat the rhino's skin in dirt, giving it extra protection against insect bites.

Terrifying tusks

This mighty male elephant will use its sharp tusks as weapons if attacked by other animals or elephants.

Tusks are very long teeth.

Animal Athletes

Which animals would make good athletes?

Imagine being able to leap straight out of water, glide through the air, or jump further than any person. Many animals use these and other amazing athletic abilities to help them survive.

Tigers can knock over prey with

Perfect pouncer

Tigers are powerful hunters. They are good at jumping and can leap great distances. They have no trouble pouncing on to the backs of large prey such as cattle. They are also good swimmers.

Striped fur hides the tiger in long grass and sun-dappled forests.

Speedy swimmer

Killer whales can leap into the air. These skilful hunters are the fastest sea mammals, moving at up to 56 km/h.

Animals that are hunted and eaten by other animals are called **prey**.

Graceful glider

Flying geckos glide from tree to tree to escape danger. Flaps of skin on the sides of their bodies act like built-in parachutes.

Skin flap

their massive paws.

Rapid runner

Although roadrunners can fly, these long-legged birds usually sprint across the ground, chasing prey or avoiding enemies.

At full speed, kangaroos bounce along on only their big back feet.

Strong back legs for leaping

Did you know? Siberian tigers are the biggest cats and can weigh as much as five men.

Born bounder

Kangaroos bound across grasslands to find plants to graze. They can leap up to 12 m – about one and a half times the human long-jump record.

To **graze** is to eat growing grass and plants.

Crafty Disguises

Some clever creatures are safely hidden from their enemies because their skin colour or markings match their surroundings. This type of disguise is called camouflage. It also helps animals to sneak up on prey.

Why do animals look the way they do?

Hidden hunter

A snowy owl's mottled brown and white feathers hide it in its Arctic habitat. This helps the owl to surprise lemmings, hares, and other prey.

Thick coat of feathers for warmth

Did you know? Chameleons can change colour to match their surroundings. Temperature or mood also affects their colour.

Feathery feet stop toes from freezing

Creative crab

A decorator crab covers itself with pieces of moss, seaweed, and sponge. This inventive disguise hides the crab on the seabed.

Amazing mimic

Some animals, such as this cricket, look so much like their surroundings that predators never notice them. Would you?

The decoration is held on by tiny bristles.

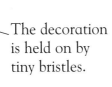

An animal's natural living place is called its **habitat**.

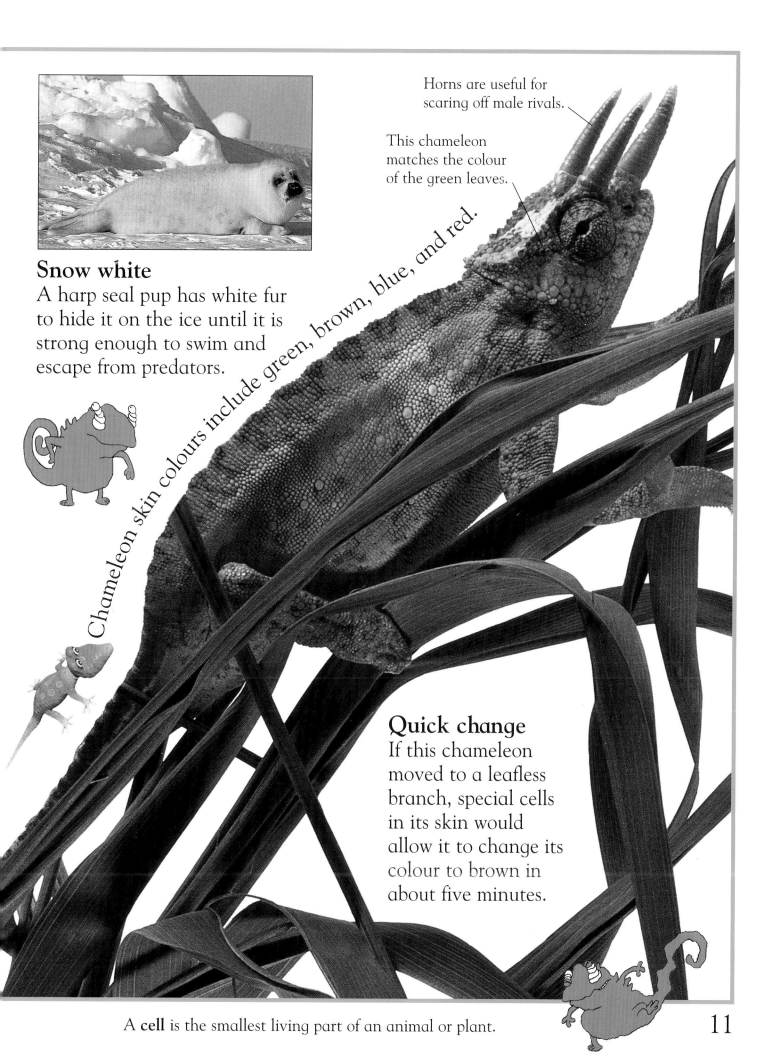

Snow white
A harp seal pup has white fur to hide it on the ice until it is strong enough to swim and escape from predators.

Horns are useful for scaring off male rivals.

This chameleon matches the colour of the green leaves.

Chameleon skin colours include green, brown, blue, and red.

Quick change
If this chameleon moved to a leafless branch, special cells in its skin would allow it to change its colour to brown in about five minutes.

A **cell** is the smallest living part of an animal or plant.

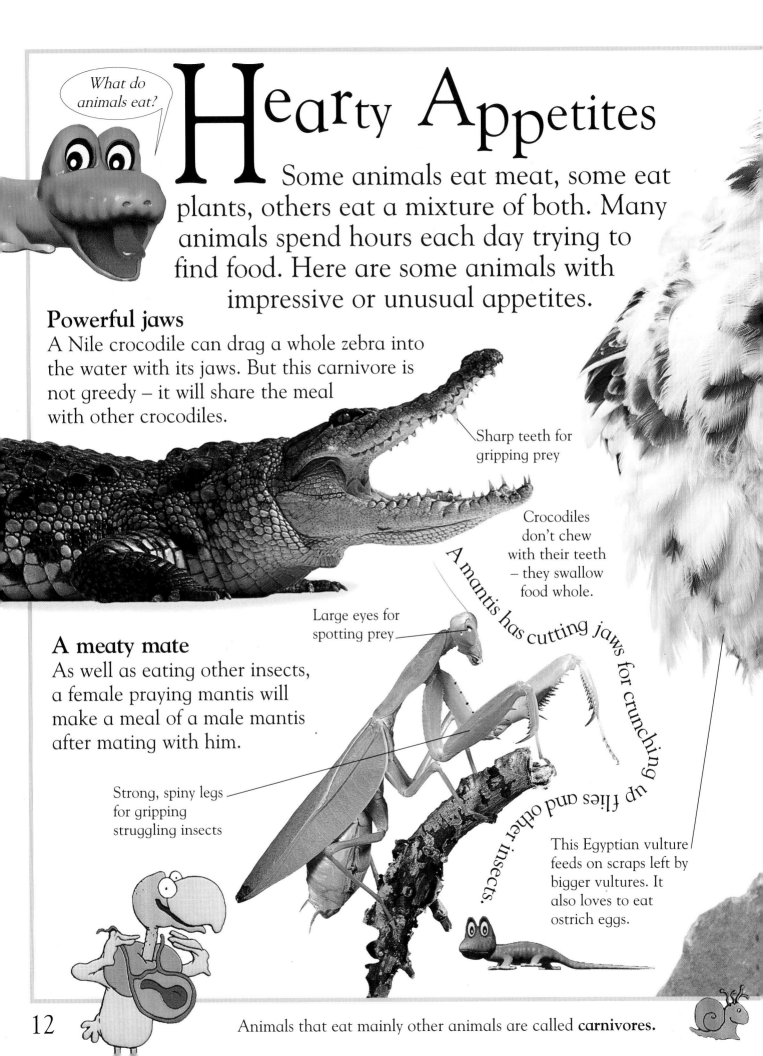

What do animals eat?

Hearty Appetites

Some animals eat meat, some eat plants, others eat a mixture of both. Many animals spend hours each day trying to find food. Here are some animals with impressive or unusual appetites.

Powerful jaws

A Nile crocodile can drag a whole zebra into the water with its jaws. But this carnivore is not greedy – it will share the meal with other crocodiles.

Sharp teeth for gripping prey

Crocodiles don't chew with their teeth – they swallow food whole.

A mantis has cutting jaws for crunching up flies and other insects.

A meaty mate

As well as eating other insects, a female praying mantis will make a meal of a male mantis after mating with him.

Large eyes for spotting prey

Strong, spiny legs for gripping struggling insects

This Egyptian vulture feeds on scraps left by bigger vultures. It also loves to eat ostrich eggs.

Animals that eat mainly other animals are called **carnivores**.

Living on leftovers

Vultures feed on dead animals. They eat everything except the bones, ripping off flesh with their sharp, curved beaks.

Sometimes vultures eat so much that they can't fly.

Did you know?
Up to 100 vultures can feed together at a time.

Healthy diet

The largest ape, the gorilla, is a peaceful herbivore. Its big belly is full of bulky food such as fruit, leaves, and roots.

A camel with only one hump is called a dromedary.

Desert hoarder

Camels are suited to desert life. They eat desert plants, store fat in their humps, and can go without a drink for long periods. People use them to carry loads across the desert.

Spread-out toes stop the camel sinking into sand.

Animals that eat mainly plants are called **herbivores.**

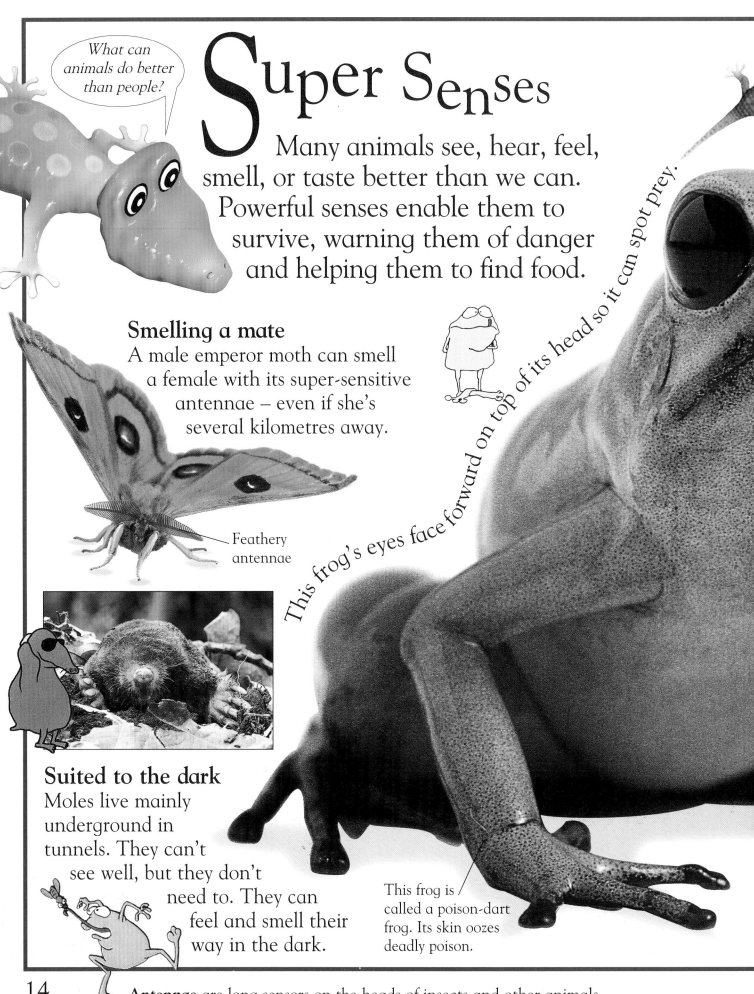

What can animals do better than people?

Super Senses

Many animals see, hear, feel, smell, or taste better than we can. Powerful senses enable them to survive, warning them of danger and helping them to find food.

Smelling a mate

A male emperor moth can smell a female with its super-sensitive antennae – even if she's several kilometres away.

Feathery antennae

This frog's eyes face forward on top of its head so it can spot prey.

Suited to the dark

Moles live mainly underground in tunnels. They can't see well, but they don't need to. They can feel and smell their way in the dark.

This frog is called a poison-dart frog. Its skin oozes deadly poison.

Antennae are long sensors on the heads of insects and other animals.

Feet taste buds

Flies can taste with their feet, so it's easy for them to find food when they land.

Bats see perfectly well – so don't say "blind as a bat".

Listening for supper

An insect-eating bat hunts by echolocation. When its squeaks bounce off an insect, the bat knows where to catch its prey.

Did you know? Frogs have long, sticky tongues for catching insects.

Upright ears help wolves to work out where a sound is coming from.

Sound sense

Can you imagine having ears sensitive enough to hear a watch ticking ten metres away? That's how well wolves hear.

This frog is only about as long as your middle finger.

Eye spy a fly

Large eyes help frogs and toads look out for tasty insects – and for danger.

Finding objects by making a sound and listening to its echo is called **echolocation.**

Why are some animals poisonous?

Powerful Poisons

Poisonous animals use their venom to kill prey or keep enemies at bay. These creatures are often tiny, yet incredibly dangerous.

Bad skin

The skin on a fire salamander's body and tail contains strong poison that protects it from hungry predators.

Poison gland

Stabbing stingers

A sea anemone's tentacles are armed with stingers. It waves them about, waiting to sting and eat passing fish. Only clownfish are safe from the poison. They are covered in protective slime.

Sea anemone

Clownfish live safely with sea anemones. Other creatures can't attack them as they risk being stung.

Fangs are pointed teeth that can be filled with poison.

Fatal fangs

A rattlesnake bites its victim with deadly fangs. It senses prey by heat, so it can hunt in the dark.

Poison from an animal is also called **venom**.

The Gila's patterned skin warns other animals to keep away.

Gilas throw their heads up and snort when threatened.

These lizards have long, sharp claws for burrowing in the desert.

Toxic chew

The Gila monster is one of only two poisonous lizards. Its venom comes from its mouth and the monster chews it into its victims.

Only about ten spiders out of 30,000 have poisons that are deadly to people.

Fast killer

Take a really good look at this Australian funnelweb spider – a bite from its fangs could kill you in less than two hours.

The rattlesnake gets its name from rattling segments at the end of its tail to scare enemies.

Did you know? Poisonous animals are often immune to their own venom.

Baby Beasts

Just like us, most animals need to be taken care of until they are grown up. Their mothers teach them how to survive.

How do baby animals learn to survive?

Babies aboard!

Baby scorpions walk after about two weeks. Until then, they travel around safely on their mothers' backs.

The baby scorpions cling to their mother.

Tiger playtime

Like many young mammals, tiger cubs play to build up their strength for adult life. These 12-week-old white tiger cubs cannot hunt yet. Their mother brings them food.

White tigers have been bred in zoos, but are very rare in the wild.

Baby gorillas have white tail tufts to help their mothers keep an eye on them.

Some young mammals, such as baby tigers and bears, are called **cubs**.

Safe seat
Gorillas walk at six months, but their mothers carry them on long trips until they're about two and a half.

Thick down keeps baby king penguins warm in the Antarctic.

Balls of fluff
Fluffy baby penguins can't swim until they grow waterproof feathers. Their parents bring them fish.

Snug home
Like other marsupials, a wallaby grows up safely in its mother's pouch, feeding on her milk. At four months it starts to hop about.

A baby wallaby is called a joey.

This cuckoo chick is waiting to be fed by its adopted mother.

Bird to adopt
A mother cuckoo doesn't bring up her chick. She lays her egg in another bird's nest and leaves it there to hatch.

Did you know? Gorillas sleep in nests built in trees or on the ground.

To **hatch** is to be born by coming out of an egg.

Record Breakers

Animals come in all shapes and sizes, from the biggest mammal – the blue whale, to the smallest insect – the fairyfly wasp. Here are more animal facts.

What's the biggest living creature?

Cicadas can be heard up to 400 m away.

Cicadas are the loudest insects.

Ostriches are the largest birds, weighing up to 156 kg.

African elephants are the heaviest animals on land.

African elephants weigh about 5,000 kg.

Giraffes are the tallest animals.

Giraffes measure up to 5.9 m tall.

Blue whales measure up to 34 m long – that's about as long as three buses.

Humans live longer than any other mammal.

Humans live up to 120 years. Asian elephants come next, living up to 90 years.

Dwarf gobies are the smallest fish at just 7.6 mm.

Eagle owls weigh about 4 kg.

Cheetahs run at up to 105 km/h over short distances.

Eagle owls are the largest owls in the world.

Cheetahs are the fastest animals on land.

Dragonflies are the fastest-flying insects.

Anacondas are the longest snakes at up to 10.26 m.

These insects can fly about 50 km/h.

Fairyfly wasps are just 0.2 mm long.